MW01487469

CONTEMPLATIVE
MEDITATION WITH
SCRIPTURE

Other Titles in This Series

CONTEMPLATIVE MEDITATION WITH SCRIPTURE

Joel S. Goldsmith

Acropolis Books, Publisher
Longboat Key, Florida

Contemplative Meditation with Scripture
by Joel S. Goldsmith

From Chapter 17 of Collected Essays of Joel S. Goldsmith,
© 1986 Thelma McDonald.

All rights reserved. This publication may not be
reproduced, copied or distributed without the express
written permission of Acropolis Books, Inc.

Acropolis Books, Inc.
Longboat Key, Florida
www.acropolisbooks.com

Except the Lord build the house,
they labour in vain that build it.

Psalm 127

Illumination dissolves all material ties and binds men together with the golden chains of spiritual understanding; it acknowledges only the leadership of the Christ; it has no ritual or rule but the divine, impersonal universal Love; no other worship than the inner Flame that is ever lit at the shrine of Spirit. This union is the free state of spiritual brotherhood. The only restraint is the discipline of Soul; therefore, we know liberty without license; we are a united universe without physical limits; a divine service to God without ceremony or creed. The illumined walk without fear – by Grace.

From the *The Infinite Way* by Joel S. Goldsmith

CONTEMPLATIVE MEDITATION WITH SCRIPTURE

CONTEMPLATIVE MEDITATION is the preparatory step before pure meditation without words or thoughts, and its main purpose is to keep the mind stayed on God—to acknowledge Him in all our ways—so that in quietness and in confidence we may "be still, and know that I am God."[1]

We know that "the natural man receiveth not the things of the Spirit of God: for they are foolishness unto him: neither can he know them, because they are spiritually discerned."[2] Therefore, only in contemplative meditation, conscious of scriptural truth, can we prepare

ourselves to attain our divine sonship or the
Buddha mind. It is promised: "If ye abide in
me, and my words abide in you, ye shall ask
what ye will, and it shall be done unto you."[3]
In other words, if we abide in the Word and
if we let the Word abide in us, we will bear
fruit richly.

Thus contemplating truth, we attain the gift
of discernment through which we attain that
truth which the 'natural man" cannot know.
This is affirmed in the Bhagavad-Gita. "See
Me! Thou canst not! nor, with human eyes,
Arjuna! Therefore I give thee sense divine.
Have other eyes, new light! And look! This is
My glory unveiled to mortal sight!"[4]

To meditate properly—to develop the ability
to practice meditation—it is necessary to
understand certain spiritual principles of
life. Unless a meditation has in it a conscious
awareness of a spiritual principle, it will

not be beneficial. It can in fact lead to just a mental stillness in which there is no spiritual fruitage or "signs following." Therefore, you must not only know why you are meditating, but you must know specific principles to take into your meditation.

Let us take the major principle of life upon which a harmonious existence can be experienced: I am *I*. Declare this to yourself, because it is indisputable. You are not someone else: you are yourself! "I am *I*." In the great lesson on supply taught in Chapter 17 of 1 Kings, when Elijah asked the poor widow to bring him a morsel of bread, she went and did according to his saying, even though she had but a handful of meal and a little oil in a cruse, "and she, and he, and her house, did eat many days." He did not inquire of her what she had or what she needed. His whole attitude was, "What do you *already* have in your house?"

Let us see how this can be applied in practical experience. When many of us are gathered together in spiritual awareness, it is easy to feel the peace among us. There is quietness and confidence, and certainly there is an absence of hate, bigotry, bias, or jealousy. Let us now ask ourselves this question: "How did this peace get here and how were bias, bigotry, and hatred eliminated?" The answer is clear. We brought into this atmosphere the peace that is here. Whatever stillness and confidence is present—whatever love is with us—we brought it. Whatever of hatred, jealousy, or discord is not here, we did not bring into our presence.

What have you in your house? What have you in your consciousness? You have love, you have life, you have cooperativeness and you have peace. What did you bring into this temple? This temple is the temple of God, but what made it so? Your being here in an atmosphere of love and mutuality. Then it is not that this room is the temple of God: it is that you are the temple of God! "Know ye not that ye are the temple of God?"[5] Ye are the temple of God *if* so be you left your personal feelings outside, *if* so be you left human limitations of anger, fear, and jealousy outside, if so be you brought in your consciousness the love and the peace we feel here. Because we *do* feel it, and because we are cognizant of the peace that is in our midst, we know beyond measure that you brought it. In other words the degree of peace, love, and joy we feel—the degree of healing consciousness that is with us—is the degree that you brought here in your consciousness.

There can be no greater degree of healing consciousness than that which you brought with you; there can be no greater degree of health than that which you brought with you; there can be no greater degree of supply than what you brought with you; and how much you brought with you depends on howmuch truth you know in your consciousness, what constitutes your consciousness, and who you are and what your true identity is.

The Master Christ Jesus asked: "Whom do men say that I am?" If the men are just human beings with no spiritual discernment, they will say that he is a Hebrew prophet, or a resurrected Hebrew prophet, or someone brought down from the human past. But "Whom say *ye* that I am?" and Peter replied: "Thou art the Christ, the Son of the living God."[6] When Peter answered the Master, he was revealing your true identity and mine, and when Christ Jesus said, "Call no man your father upon the earth: for one is your Father, which is in heaven,"[7] he was referring to your consciousness and my consciousness. As a matter of fact, his entire ministry was a revelation of man's spiritual *sonship*. Therefore, you can bring infinite peace, infinite harmony, infinite healing consciousness, and infinite supply into a group of people, but you can accomplish this in only one way, by knowing that "I and my Father are one,"[8] and "Son, thou art ever with me, and all that I have is thine."[9]

Think what would happen if you set aside ten minutes every morning to be separate and apart from the outside world for the purpose of contemplating God and the things of God. Think what would happen should you set aside ten minutes for spiritual realization! Only those who have been touched in some measure by the Spirit of God would have the capacity to sit for ten minutes in contemplative meditation. Think!

"I and my Father are one." The Father has said to me, "Son, thou art ever with me, and all that I have is thine." Therefore, I have all that God has; all that God has is mine. "The earth is the Lord's, and the fulness thereof."[10] Of my own self I am nothing but, in this oneness with my Father, all that the Father hath is mine. "My peace I give unto you."[11] There is no limitation to the amount of peace that I have, because I have been given the Christ peace, the My peace. The Christ peace has been given unto me.

Therefore, when the question is asked, "What have you in your house?" you can reply: "I have the full measure of Christ peace. I have all that the Father has, for the Father has given His allness unto me. God has even breathed into me His life, so I have in my consciousness life eternal. The Christ has come that I might have life, and that I might have it abundantly. Therefore, I have in my house—in my consciousness—abundant life, infinite life, eternal life, because this Christ has said, 'I am eternal life.' Therefore, I have eternal life in my consciousness as the gift of God. I have an infinity of supply because the Christ reveals: 'Your heavenly Father knoweth that ye have need of all these things,'[12] and 'it is your Father's good pleasure to give you the kindgom.'[13] Therefore, I have the kingdom of God within me, which is the kingdom of all that I shall ever need. I have in my consciousness eternal life, infinite supply, divine peace. The peace which passeth understanding I have."

As you contemplate these principles for five or ten minutes each day, you carry into your world the awareness of the presence of all that God is and all that God has as a gift that has been bestowed upon you by the grace of God.

Your having contemplated these truths is the reason there is peace in our midst. You have brought "the peace of God, which passeth all understanding."[14] If there is love here with us, you have brought the love that is without limit. If there is supply, you have brought God's storehouse. All that the Father has is yours, and you have brought it here. Remember this: What you have brought here to make of this room a temple of God, you also bring to your business or to your home by your morning contemplation of this truth. You thereby make of your home a temple of God. You do not find love in your home: you bring love to your home, because love is found only where you express it. In other words, if your family is to find love, they will find it because you, who are attuned to God, bring it there. You who have been led to a spiritual teaching have been given the grace to know this truth, whereas members of your family and your business associates who are represented by "the natural man who receiveth not the things of God" cannot bring peace and harmony into their relationships.

Only those who have the Spirit of God indwelling are children of God. Only those who have the Spirit of God indwelling have been given the "peace which passeth understanding." Therefore, remember: What you discover here at this moment you have brought. Likewise, what you find in your home, in your business, in the world is what you bring to your home, to your business, or to the world.

What have you in your consciousness? This is the password for meditation: "What have I in my consciousness?"

Of myself I have nothing, but by the grace of God "all things that the Father hath are mine[15] *... the*

earth, is the Lord's, and the fulness thereof."[16]
Therefore, I have been given My peace, the Christ
peace. I have been given all these added things
because my heavenly Father knoweth that I have
need of them and it is His good pleasure to fulfill
me. I am filled full of the grace of God and, by the
grace of God, all that the Father hath is mine.

If you ask Me, I can give you bread; eating it, you
will never hunger. I can give you living waters;
drinking, you will never thirst.

This is what you are saying in your household,
in your business, in the world—only you
are saying it silently and secretly. You never
voice it openly because the command of the
Master is that we do our praying in secret,
where no man can hear us or see us. If your
praying is done in the inner sanctuary of
your consciousness, what the Father seeth
or heareth in secret is shouted from the
housetops. "Thy Father which seeth in secret
himself shall reward thee openly."[17] Silently

and sacredly ask yourself: "What have I in the house?"

I have the grace of God. All that the Father hath is mine. I have been given quietness and confidence and stillness; I have been given My peace. The Father hath breathed His life into me, therefore I have God's life which is eternal and immortal.

I have that mind in me which was also in Christ Jesus, and so I have no human desires and I seek nothing of any man. "I and my Father are one," and I receive all that I require because my Father knoweth my needs, and it is His good pleasure to give me the kingdom. Because I already have all, I pray only for the opportunity to share that which the Father hath given to me.

Note what transpires in your home, in your business, and in the world as you silently, sacredly, and secretly remind yourself:

Thank God I ask nothing of any man except that we love one another. I ask only the privilege of sharing God's allness which is already mine. Why should I look to "man, whose breath is in his nostrils,"[18] *wher by right of divine sonship I am heir to all of the heavenly riches!*

Do you not see why there is an atmosphere of peace among us? We came here for the purpose of abiding in the presence of God and to tabernacle with the Spirit of God which is within you and within me. We are gathered together to share the spiritual grace of God, the spiritual presence of God and the spiritual love of God. That is why there is peace with us; there can be no such peace where people come to *get* something. When you sit down to meditate, turn quietly within and realize:

As the branch is one with the tree, as the wave is one with the ocean, so am I one with God. The allness of Infinity is pouring Itself forth into expression as my individual being, as my individual consciousness, as my individual life. Having received the allness of God, I want only to share it.

14

As you resume your outer activity, you remember to have a ten-second meditation as often as possible, in which to remind yourself:

The grace of God is upon me. I have spiritual meat and spiritual bread to share with all who are here, and those who accept it will never hunger. I can give to the world spiritual water, and those who accept this living water will never thirst. "I and my Father are one," and the Father is pouring Its allness through me, to you, and to this world.

A contemplative meditation has in it something of a back-and-forth nature. You are virtually saying to the Father:

Thank You, Father, that Your grace is upon me. Thank You, Father, that You have given me Your peace. If I have any hope, or faith, or confidence, You have given it to me. Of my own self I am nothing, so whatever measure of peace, hope, faith, and confidence I have is the gift of the Father within me. Thank You, Father, for Your grace, Your peace, Your abundance.

15

You then pause, as if the still small voice were about to speak to you. It is an attitude of "Speak, Lord; for thy servant heareth."[19] If you persist in this way of life, eventually you will discover that the Father *will* speak to you, and usually in this manner:

Son, I have been with you since before Abraham was. Know ye not that "I am with you alway, even unto the end of the world"?[20] Know ye not that "I will never leave thee, nor forsake thee"?[21] If you mount up to heaven, I will be there with you. Turn and recognize Me even in hell. If you walk through the valley of the shadow of death, I will not leave you.

Turn within and seek Me. Acknowledge Me in the midst of you, and I will change death into life, age into youth, lack into abundance. Only abide in this Word and consciously let Me abide in you. Whither do you think you can flee from My Spirit!

Open your consciousness and feel the peace which passes understanding where you are.

My peace give I unto you—My peace. My kingdom, the kingdom of Allness, is established within you. Abide in this truth and let this truth abide in you. Consciously remember that the son of God indwells you and that It is closer to you than breathing and nearer than hands and feet. "I can do all things through Christ which strengthened me.[22] ... I live; yet not I, but Christ liveth in me."[23] Let Me, this indwelling son of God, abide in you.

If you have been led to a spiritual way of life, you will not have the capability to forget your ten-second meditations and your ten-minute contemplative meditations. If the Spirit of God dwells in you, you will be as unable to go through the hours of the day and night without the conscious remembrance of the presence of God as you would be unable to go without food. As food is necessary to the "natural man," so the conscious awareness of the presence of God is vital to the spiritual man. Spiritual food is essential to the son of God.

Silently and secretly make this acknowledgment to your family, to your business acquaintances, and to your neighbors: "I can give you living waters." Witness to what degree this changes the trend of your thought from being the "man of earth" who is always seeking to get something to being the spiritual son of God who is motivated by the desire to give and to share: "Ask of me, and I can give you the peace that passeth understanding. I can share with you the indwelling Christ peace which the Father hath given me."

Witness how this reverses the trend of your life. Whereas the natural man receiveth not the things of God because he is too busy seeking the baubles of "this world," the spiritual man is not only always receiving but he is sharing. He is able to discern that these spiritual treasures cannot be hoarded: they must always be expressed and allowed to flow from the within to the without. And so you secretly and sacredly carry them into your home and into your business, and then you take the next step and let them flow to your enemy.

"Father, forgive them; for they know not what they do."[24] *If you ask Me, I will give you living waters, and you will never thirst again. I will give you meat, and you will never again hunger. I am come that you might have life, and that you might have it more abundantly.*

As you practice contemplative meditation, think what is pouring through you to this world to help establish peace on earth. There has not been peace on earth because so many individuals have been seeking it, and few there are who have sought to bring it, to express it, to share it. If there is to be peace on earth, the Master clearly reveals that you and I must bring it—and this *I* is the *I* of you, the divine

Son of you. If there is to be peace in the world, *you* must bring it—just as you brought it here and as you are learning to carry it into your home and into your business activity. Peace is not here until you bring it. What have you in your consciousness?

I have the peace that passeth understanding, and I can carry it wherever I will, wherever I am, because in God's presence there is fulfillment. The place whereon I stand is holy ground because Christ dwelleth in me. The indwelling Christ is the fulfillment, and where the Christ is there is peace. Therefore I bring peace to my body, I bring peace and quiet to my mind, and I bring peace, quiet, love, and abundance to you, whoever the "you" may be. I bring to you the grace of God. Go thou and do likewise!

1. Psalm 46:10

2. I Corinthians 2:14

3. John 15:7

4. The Song Celestial, trans. Sir Edwin Arnold (London:Routledge and Kegan Paul), p. 63

5. I Corinthians 3:16

6. Matthew 16:13, 15, 16

7. Matthew 23:9

8. John 10:30

9. Luke 15:31

10. Psalm 24:1

11. John 14:27

12. Matthew 6:32

13. Luke 12:32

14. Philippians 4:7

15. John 16:15

16. Psalm 24:1

17. Matthew 6:4

18. Isaiah 2:22

19. 1 Samuel 3:9

20. Matthew 28:20

21. Hebrews 13:5

22. Philippians 4:13

23. Galatians 2:20

24. Luke 23:34

Printed in Great Britain
by Amazon